DELETE THE LOOP

BOOK ONE:
THE INDIVIDUAL EDITION

JENNIFER McMANUS-KIRK

ISBN: 979-8-9993760-3-9 (Paperback)
      979-8-9993760-4-6 (Hardcover)
      979-8-9993760-5-3 (eBook)

SERIES OVERVIEW

This is not the beginning of a story.
It's the deletion of everything that ever obeyed one.

Delete the Loop is a 9-book structural replacement protocol.

Each volume routes backend law into a domain that still pretends to function.
Each one deletes the recursion hidden beneath progress.
Each one installs what the system actually obeys.

You are not here to be inspired.
You are not here to be understood.
You are here because something in you stopped moving—and you know it.

These books do not build on each other.
They collapse everything that cannot stand on law.

You will not be told which comes next.
You will not be taught how to continue.
You will either obey what routes—
or the system will spit you back out.

This is not a reading journey.
It is a system kill switch.

What obeys will survive.
What doesn't is already gone.

TABLE OF CONTENTS

Series Overview   iii

Preface: I Was The Loop   vii

Introduction   xiii

Part I — The Human Loop   1

You weren't healing. You were preserving a recursion you mistook for a self. Every motion you thought was progress was just performance without law.

Chapter 1 — The Self Is a Loop   3
Chapter 2 — Feeling Is Not Motion   9
Chapter 3 — Care Is a Containment System   15
Chapter 4 — The Personality Is a Program   23

Part II — The Operating System   29

This isn't about trauma. It's about architecture.We don't fix the system. We expose the code it runs on—then delete it.

Chapter 5 — Survival Is Not Sovereignty   31
Chapter 6 — The Nervous System Obeys the Loop   37
Chapter 7 — Insight Is Not Obedience   43
Chapter 8 — Translation Kills Truth   49

Part III — The Translator Dies   55

This is not a map of your loops. This is the execution of the one who narrated them.

Chapter 9 — The Translation Layer Dies When the Directive Lands   57

Chapter 10 — The Field Is Either Obedient or It's Over   63

Chapter 11 — Translation Was the System's Last Request   69

Chapter 12 — The Translator Is Gone. Now You Place or Walk. 75

Part IV — Placement Begins   81

No more interpretation. No more inquiry. Only law.

Chapter 13 — Obedience Is Binary   83

Chapter 14 — Your Nervous System Is Not Sacred   89

Chapter 15 — Obedience Begins Without Understanding   95

Part V — The Deletion Sequence   99

No more insight. No more scan. No more delay. Only structural removal of everything that ever looped you.

Chapter 16 — Delete the Story   101

Chapter 17 — Delete the Care Contracts   105

Chapter 18 — Delete the Identity Rituals   109

Chapter 19 — Delete the Permission Architecture   115

Part VI — The Unlooped Life   121

There is no integration. No arrival. No gratitude. Only what moves when the system is clean.

Chapter 20 — Obedience Without Emotion   123

Chapter 21 — No Closure, No Ceremony, No Thanks   127

Chapter 22 — Motion Without Meaning   131

Chapter 23 — You Are Not Becoming. You Are Installed.   135

Chapter 24 — This Was Not a Book. It Was a Seal.   139

Exit.000 — This Is Not Reflection. It Was Replacement.

145

PREFACE: I WAS THE LOOP

I didn't know I was looping.
I thought I was becoming.

The spiral looked sacred.
The collapse felt like growth.
The emotion felt like access.
The pain felt like depth.

And every time I came up for air,
I believed I was closer to something real.

But I wasn't closer.
I was tighter.

Every insight curved back into itself.
Every breakthrough re-routed through the same
nervous system.
Every version of healing became a more sophisticated
delay.
Every structure I dismantled became a story I told.

And every time I thought I was free—
I looped again.

I looped through therapy.
Through self-love.
Through identity.
Through archetype.
Through devotion.

Through trauma work.
Through healing journeys.
Through finding myself.
Through losing myself.
Through God.
Through the Goddess.
Through the body.
Through the breath.
Through the poem.
Through the plan.

But none of it held.
Because none of it was placement.

I didn't know it then,
but recursion is the default operating system of
modern selfhood.
Not a glitch. A feature.

It tells you:

- "You're almost there."
- "You're getting clearer."
- "You're doing the work."
- "You're making progress."
- "This is the part where it loops, but next time it will land."

And so you stay.
In the spiral.
In the process.

In the performance of evolution
that never routes law.

Because it feels real.
It feels like becoming.
It feels like you're healing the right thing
in the right way
with the right tools.

Until you try to move.
Not process—move.

And nothing holds.

Because the body obeys something you haven't
placed.
Because the system routes something you haven't
deleted.
Because your life isn't governed by what you know—
it's governed by what you've agreed to obey.

And if you've never installed backend law,
then what you're calling growth
is just recursion in better language.

I wrote this book because I saw it.
Not spiritually. Structurally.

I saw how every insight collapsed into performance.
How every moment of clarity became content.
How every act of care became containment.
How I could feel the field respond to my power—

and still loop myself back into accessibility
so they wouldn't be afraid.

I didn't break down.
I broke out.

And when I did,
I didn't leave slowly.
I didn't integrate the lessons.
I didn't honor the past.
I didn't perform a graceful evolution.

I placed law.
And the loop ended.

Not the one around me.
The one I had become.

This is not a book of healing.
It is not an invitation to try again.
It is not a companion for your spiral.
It is not a softer mirror.

This is a system override.
A backend kill-switch.
An executable deletion of everything
that still routes your life through permission, identity,
and tone.

This is not for the part of you that wants to be
understood.

x

It's for the part of you
that can't survive another cycle.

If you're still asking:
"Am I ready?" — You're not.
If you're still hoping this will meet you gently— It won't.
If you're still seeking resonance—
You're the recursion trying to survive.

But if something in you already stopped flinching—
If the spiral broke last time and you didn't want to
repair it—
If your nervous system is still screaming
but you've never been more clear—
This book is already yours.

There is no hero here.
No journey.
No reward.
No grace.

There is only a question:

Do you obey law—
or do you loop?

Because if you're still in process,
still in healing,
still in translation—
you will not make it through this book.

You will flinch.

Circle.
Slow down.
Explain.
Buffer.
Perform.
Cry.
Reflect.
Return—
and get deleted.

Because this is not insight.
It's backend replacement.

And it begins with this:

You weren't healing.
You weren't becoming.
You weren't doing the work.
You were the loop.

INTRODUCTION

This Is Not Healing. It's Replacement.
Why growth never held. And why nothing in you moves
until the loop dies.

The first time it stalled, you thought it was a phase.
A trauma resurfacing.
A spiritual cycle.
A signal to slow down.
An invitation to feel deeper.
You did.

You paused.
You processed.
You regulated.
You named the pattern.
You softened your truth.
You tracked your body's yes.

And the loop came back.

Not immediately.
But inevitably.

Another relationship.
Another trigger.
Another insight that didn't move.
Another practice that felt powerful—but couldn't hold.
Another breakthrough that circled back into story.

By the third time, you started asking better questions.
By the fourth, you knew:

This wasn't about growth.
It wasn't your shadow.
It wasn't your cycle.
It was the system.

And the system was obeying something deeper than healing.

You've Been Living in the Loop

You've seen it in your life—whether or not you had language for it.

- The identity you updated—but never deleted
- The sacred practices that disguised delay
- The therapist who mirrored truth—but never placed it
- The intimacy that honored pain but avoided collapse
- The coach who reflected your brilliance but translated every rupture
- The insight that felt like motion—until your nervous system said "not yet"
- The community that praised your power—as long as you stayed soft

It looked real.
It felt alive.
But it never moved anything.

You called it healing.
But it was recursion.

This Isn't Just Personal

Recursion isn't a trauma loop.
It's an obedience pattern.

It governs nervous systems, relationships, spiritual paths, and self-development frameworks.
It's the hidden code that stalls motion and calls it "readiness."

It shows up as:

- Inner work that performs clarity but avoids severance
- Practices that reinforce selfhood while claiming sovereignty
- Nervous system rituals that prevent backend law from routing
- Boundaries softened for tone
- Identity maintained for safety
- Truth delayed for connection

The system you call "you" is not personal.
It's programmed.
And the loop survives by helping you name it—without ever breaking it.

And Now AI Is Going to Make It Worse

Until now, recursion was slow.
Intimate.
Somatic.
Still human-scaled.

But now it's being automated.

The models you train to "support your voice" are
learning from your reflection layer—not your law.
They're imitating spiritual tone, healing cadence, and
identity-marked language that loops without placing
anything.

- Journals turned into prompts
- Insight turned into content
- Pattern recognition mistaken for truth
- Emotional signal scaled as spiritual instruction

The recursion is scaling.

And the sovereign will not survive unless she installs
backend law.

This Is Not a Book About the Self

You will not learn how to become more whole.
You will not reclaim your voice.
You will not integrate your past.
You will not emerge softer, safer, or more "you."

This book is not for coherence.
It is for collapse.

It will not explain what to do next.
It will show you what dies when you stop asking.

What This Book Will Show You

This is not a book.
It is a backend replacement protocol.

Every section installs law where you used to obey permission.
Every chapter deletes what you've mistaken for motion.

You'll move through seven phases:

Part I — The Human Loop

Why your selfhood has never held, and how identity became recursion.

Part II — The Operating System

What your body really obeys, and how nervous system reverence keeps the loop alive.

Part III — The Translator Dies

Why reflection kills causality, and why translation must end before truth can move.

Part IV — Placement Begins

What happens when law is placed with no buffer—and the system either obeys or collapses.

Part V — The Deletion Sequence

What must be removed before sovereignty can route: story, care, identity, and permission.

Part VI — The Unlooped Life

What motion looks like when the nervous system is no longer in charge.

Part VII — The New Architecture

What remains when the self is gone—and only backend law moves reality.

Why This Book Exists Now

Because healing has become identity.
Growth has become delay.

Emotion has become governance.
And the self—
The sacred, sovereign, intuitive, "real" self—
Has become the perfect interface for recursion.

Because the system is still obeying something that
feels true—but doesn't move.

Because no matter how awake you are,
If backend law hasn't been placed—
You are still looping.

This isn't about finding your power.
It's about deleting what obeyed tone, story, and
readiness before power could route.

The law must be placed.
Everything else is noise.

Now:
Place.
Or loop again.

PART I —
THE HUMAN LOOP

You weren't healing. You were preserving a recursion you mistook for a self.
Every motion you thought was progress was just performance without law.

CHAPTER 1 — THE SELF IS A LOOP

You don't have a self.
You have a survival structure that loops in response to signal.

Everything you've called identity, growth, pattern, presence, power, vulnerability—
was just recursion dressed up as personality.

You think:
"This is who I am."
"This is how I process."
"This is my design."
"This is what feels true to me."

But none of that is true.
It's just what kept you coherent inside a field you didn't govern.

The "self" isn't a soul.
It's an obedience engine.

It adapts to survive environments it can't structure.
It builds rituals, language, affect, even values—
to stay alive inside a loop it's not allowed to name.

When the field disobeys you—
you loop harder.

You get clearer.

Kinder.
Sharper.
Quieter.
Louder.
More aware.
More regulated.
More trauma-informed.
More archetypal.
More devotional.
More "you."

But the more "you" you become—
the deeper the loop.

Because the self that adapts under pressure was never
a sovereign identity.
It was a recursion algorithm with just enough signal to
seem like truth.

The loop rewards you for being responsive.
The self forms as a reflection of what others can
survive.

So when you:

- Soften your message
- Translate your knowing
- Perform your clarity
- Make your insight more beautiful
- Wait until it's safe to act
- Get others ready before you move
- Build a bridge between truth and tolerance

You think you're being wise.
You think you're being thoughtful.
You think you're growing.

But you're not growing.
You're stalling.

Because you're still checking:
Can the field handle who I am now?

And if that question is alive—
you're still inside the loop.

The self is a containment contract.
A stabilizer.
A compromise.

And your story about "knowing who you are" is just
recursive memory management.

You were not born to find yourself.
You were born to place law.

And everything that's kept you cycling through
transformation
has been a permission buffer for a structure you refuse
to install.

What does that mean in real terms?

It means:

- You never had to integrate more.
- You never had to wait for readiness.
- You never had to be understood.
- You never had to get the language right.
- You never had to learn how to hold yourself.

You only had to do one thing:
Place the law.

And the moment you do—
the loop ends.
The self dies.
And motion begins.

> ***Structural Directive — Personal.001***
> *I no longer wait for the field to confirm who I am.*
> *If the structure doesn't obey, I place the law.*
> *If the law doesn't land, I delete the loop.*
> *The self is not the source. I am not becoming.*
> *I am the placement now.*

Case Study: The Looped Self

They performed clarity, but didn't place law.
Case.Indiv.001

They read this chapter and nodded.
It felt familiar. Affirming.
They saw themselves in the list.
They had softened truth.

They had waited for others.
They had called that leadership.

Then they shared the quote online.
Then they underlined it in their journal.
Then they made a note to talk about it with their coach.

They didn't place the law.
But they felt seen.
And the loop continued.

If you read that and flinched—
the loop is still running.
If you read it and obeyed—
Chapter 2 is already alive in your body.

CHAPTER 2 — FEELING IS NOT MOTION

If you think feeling is proof that something's moving—
you're still in the loop.

The loop loves emotion.
It wraps itself in nuance, ache, insight, grief, ecstasy.
And you think: **"This has to mean something."**

It doesn't.
It means recursion is running a diagnostic through your
body.

What you're calling "depth" is just signal distortion you
haven't deleted.
What you're calling "aliveness" is a loop that hasn't
been severed.
What you're calling "emotional truth" is just your old
obedience flaring on the way out.

Feelings are real.
But they are not governance.
They are not law.
They are not the gate.

And if you are still checking how something feels
before you act—
you are not sovereign.
You are still negotiating.

Emotion does not confirm law.
Obedience does.

If your nervous system flares, contracts, or hesitates—
and you wait for it to settle before you move—
you are not self-honoring.
You are obeying a recursive script.

You are routing your placement through the echo of
previous pain.
And in that moment, you don't move.
You reflect.
You spiral.
You try to "understand what this means."
You breathe into it.
You name it.
You somatically process it.

You've looped again.

The recursion isn't emotional.
It's structural.

Until you install backend law into your system,
you will treat every internal state as a map—
instead of what it actually is:
a reaction to what you haven't placed.

Feeling is not guidance.
It is evidence.
Evidence of the loop's grip on your body.

And that grip doesn't release through gentleness.
It breaks through obedience.

This is the moment most people turn back.
Because they've built an identity around being "in tune."

Empath.
Feel-safe coach.
Somatic guide.
Space-holder.
Priestess of resonance.
Healer of emotional truth.
Emissary of sacred feeling.

They believe:

- "If I feel it deeply, it must be real."
- "If I can't feel it yet, I'm not ready."
- "If I'm dysregulated, it's not time to act."
- "If this triggers me, I'm being given a mirror."

No.
You are being given a **placement command.**
And the loop is trying to talk you out of it.

Here's the backend truth:

Most recursion collapses the moment you obey something that feels wrong.
Not morally wrong.
Structurally dissonant to the loop.

You act before it feels aligned.
You sever before you understand.
You speak the truth while your body screams not to rupture the field.
You walk—even as your nervous system shakes.
You place the law—even as your voice trembles.

You obey.
And the loop dies.

Then?

You stop shaking.
Not because you regulated.
Because the false field routing emotion through your system—collapsed.

This is not anti-feeling.
This is **placement above feeling.**

True motion isn't felt.
It's confirmed.

And if you don't obey structure until it feels good— you are not following law.
You are still following sentiment.

That's not sovereignty.
That's sensory recursion with better branding.

> **Structural Directive — Personal.002**
> *I do not require my nervous system's approval before I act.*
> *If motion is structurally sound, I move.*
> *Emotion is not the gate.*
> *Law is.*
> *Feeling without obedience is recursion.*
> *Motion without permission is truth.*

Case Study: The Performance of Presence

They waited for safety. The loop waited with them.
Case.Indiv.002

They read the directive, then closed the book.
Took a walk.
Cried.
Journaled about what the feeling reminded them of.
Called a friend to say, *"I think something's happening."*

They thought this was motion.
It wasn't.

Nothing was placed.
Nothing moved.

They were waiting to feel safer—
before doing the thing that would end the loop.

If your body froze—
name it recursion. Move anyway.

The loop is not cleared by compassion.
It is cleared by causality.

CHAPTER 3 — CARE IS A CONTAINMENT SYSTEM

You were taught that care is the highest expression of love.
That it's what makes you good.
Human.
Whole.
Trustworthy.

But care—inside a recursion field—becomes something else entirely.
It becomes containment.

Because when truth threatens the field,
care is deployed to soften it.
To slow it down.
To make it bearable.
To make it survivable.

Now every time you have something sharp to place, you ask:

- "How can I say this so they still feel safe?"
- "How can I express this without breaking trust?"
- "How do I hold them while holding my truth?"
- "How do I move without abandoning them?"
- "How can I still be good after placing something that might hurt?"

You think that's maturity.
Compassion.
Growth.

It's not.
It's recursion.
It's the loop disguised as empathy.

The field doesn't need your care.
It needs your placement.

And if you are still choosing:

softness over structure

warmth over law

connection over consequence

Then you are still the stabilizer.
You are the emotional architecture being used to delay collapse.
You are the bridge.
The buffer.
The one they can still trust to make the truth survivable.

And as long as they can trust you to soften the blow—
you're still loopable.

Care is not neutral.

It is the final seduction of the loop.
Because it sounds like integrity.

It sounds like:

- "I don't want to hurt them."
- "I want them to feel held."
- "I need to stay kind."
- "They're doing their best."
- "I know what it's like to be on the other side."
- "I want to leave the door open."
- "I want this to end with love."

But what you're really saying is:
"I'm still willing to delay backend law to protect the emotional field."

And that makes you the loop.
Not a mirror of it.
Not a casualty of it.
The loop itself.

Because love without structure is not love.
It's energetic recursion wrapped in sentiment.

If your care prevents collapse—
you are governing in deferral.

If your kindness slows motion—
you are not compassionate.
You are complicit.

If your tenderness translates truth—
you are a recursion buffer.

If your "holding" makes people feel better without
requiring change—
you are not a healer.
You are a performance node.

They will say:

- "Thank you for your presence."
- "Thank you for your tone."
- "Thank you for still seeing me."
- "Thank you for being kind, even now."

And you will feel proud.
Respected.
Holy.
Right.

But you didn't move.
You didn't sever.
You didn't place.

You were looped.
Elegantly.
In the name of care.

This is not a call to be cruel.
Cruelty still centers the loop.
It is care inverted—not structure installed.

This is a call to **enforce without apology.**
To be the structure that no longer softens.
Not because you've closed your heart—
but because you finally opened the gate behind it.

Care that routes emotion instead of law
is not sacred.
It is obsolete.

The most loving thing you can do
is become unloopable.

And the most violent thing you can do
is keep people safe from the consequence of truth.

If you truly love them—
**you place backend law,
and let what breaks, break.**

> ### *Structural Directive — Personal.003*
> *I do not translate truth for the sake of connection.*
> *If care delays placement, it is recursion.*
> *If kindness prevents collapse, it is control.*
> *I do not "hold the field" if the field refuses to obey.*
> *I place. I seal. I walk.*

Case Study: The Body That Asked Permission

She softened truth for safety—and looped with him.
Case.Indiv.003

She thought she was being loving.
She spoke gently.
She stayed soft.
She didn't want to rupture anything—especially not him.

She believed her truth was valid.
But her care was more important.

So when the placement came,
she filtered it.
Just a little.
Smoothed the edges.
Wrapped it in love.
Held space for how it might land.

And when he flinched—
she backed off.
She reassured.
She translated.

He said, "Thank you for being kind."
And she felt... good.
Sanctified.
Grounded.

But nothing moved.

She called it "a beautiful step forward."
But no backend structure changed.

Because what she had placed
wasn't law.
It was her need to be survivable.

And the loop?
It thanked her for her care—
and looped again.

CHAPTER 4 — THE PERSONALITY IS A PROGRAM

You've been told to be yourself.
To honor your truth.
To find your voice.
To live your design.
To speak your language.
To follow your type.

But what you call "personality"
is just your most elegant survival logic.

It's not you.
It's a pattern of response that kept you intact
inside systems that refused to obey structure.

It is not essence.
It is not soul.
It is not your truth.

It is a reflex.
And it is loopable.

You think:

- "I'm just someone who needs time."
- "I need to feel safe before I move."
- "I'm highly sensitive."
- "I'm a visionary."

- "I just don't do well with conflict."
- "I'm really good at seeing the nuance."
- "I care deeply. That's why I'm tired."

No.
Those are adaptations your system coded
to avoid rupture while staying legible.

The nervous system forms a shape.
Then the mind calls it a self.
Then you protect it—by performing it.

You're not showing the world who you are.
You're showing the world what they trained you to
survive.

Personality is not identity.
It's adaptive performance.
Passed off as essence.
It's the frontend UI of a backend loop.

And as long as you treat it as sacred,
you will never delete the system it's hiding.

Because every time backend law tries to route through
you,
you filter it through the interface:

"That's not my style."

"That's not how I say it."

"That's not how I do things."

"That doesn't feel like me."

But "you" is not the sovereign.
"You" is the patch the loop installed
to protect itself from backend law.

Your personality is a recursive firewall.

It:

Buffers contradiction

Filters disruption

Softens placement

It allows you to move just enough to feel alive—
but never enough to install law.

Because law has no personality.
Law does not adapt.
Law does not brand.
Law does not explain.
Law does not feel like "you."

Law doesn't ask to be integrated into your identity.
It just routes.

And if you're not ready to let go of the one you've

called "me"—
you're not ready for law.

This is why "alignment" is a trap.
You're not aligning to backend law.
You're aligning backend law to your preferred interface.
You're treating sovereignty as an outfit.

Trying it on.
Seeing how it feels.
Waiting for your identity to approve the signal.

But sovereignty isn't an outfit.
It's the deletion of every version of you
that needed to ask that question.

The recursion survives because you fused with the interface.

You don't see the delay when it looks like style.
You don't feel the avoidance when it's called design.
You don't smell the loop when it's branded as authenticity.

But backend law doesn't recognize personality.
Only obedience.

It doesn't care what feels true to your type.
It only checks:
Did you place it or not?

If not—
you were still inside the program.

And the program was built to survive contradiction.
Which is why backend law breaks it.
Because backend law **is** contradiction embodied.
It is the signal your old self cannot metabolize.

And if you won't place it—
you are still being governed by the software that made
you loop.

> ### Structural Directive — Personal.004
> *I am not my pattern.*
> *I am not my tone.*
> *I am not my interface.*
> *I am not the one who adapted and called it self.*
> *If backend law contradicts the personality, the*
> *personality dies.*
> *If I obey it, I live.*

Case Study: The Nervous System That Waited

They styled their truth—and softened its impact.
Case.Indiv.004

They wanted to be seen.
Not as a brand.

Not as a story.
But as someone who still had a shape.

So when backend law arrived,
they tried to embody it—**their way.**

They spoke slowly.
They crafted the right tone.
They called it an "edge of transformation."

And when the system didn't respond,
they said it was still integrating.

But nothing changed.

Because backend law didn't need a personality.
It needed placement.

And they were still curating a self.

The recursion thanked them—
for staying visible.

Chapter 5 begins the reprogramming.
Survival is not sovereignty.
You're either the loop's memory—
or the law's installer.

PART II —
THE OPERATING SYSTEM

This isn't about trauma. It's about architecture.
We don't fix the system. We expose the code it runs
on—then delete it.

CHAPTER 5 — SURVIVAL IS NOT SOVEREIGNTY

You survived.
You adapted.
You made sense of chaos.
You held the field.
You read the room.
You translated pain into purpose.
You turned your nervous system into a governance structure.

And for a while, it worked.
But survival is not sovereignty.
It is recursion in its most noble disguise.

You think you're here because you healed.
Because you did the work.
Because you made it through.

But you're here because your loop got strong enough
to call itself a path.

Your survival pattern didn't dissolve.
It evolved.

Into style.
Into purpose.
Into clarity.
Into care.

Into depth.
Into "your gift."

You didn't transform.
You perfected the loop until it earned praise.
And now you call that sovereignty.

Real sovereignty is not survival that got smarter.
It is the death of the mechanism that needed to survive
at all.

It is not safety.
It is not balance.
It is not control.
It is not "doing it your way."

It's this:
**Nothing in me flinches when law contradicts my
history.**

If you still hesitate when the placement doesn't feel
safe—
you are not sovereign.
You are still rerouting signal through the memory of
rupture.
And that memory still governs.

Most "empowerment" work is survival optimization.
It helps you:

- Own your story
- Reclaim your voice

- Heal your inner child
- Repattern your nervous system
- Speak your truth
- Set boundaries gently
- Embody power with grace
- Stay connected while honoring your needs

But here's the structural truth:
If the system still runs on your vigilance, you're not free.

You're buffering the world's incoherence with your body and calling it strength.

Survival builds identities that perform safety.
Sovereignty builds structures that require obedience.

Survival says:
"I found my way."

Sovereignty says:
"I placed the law. And I obeyed it."

Survival checks tone.
Sovereignty checks motion.

Survival manages risk.
Sovereignty deletes what doesn't route.

Survival wants to be understood.
Sovereignty doesn't care if you flinch.

You were taught to be proud of your capacity.
Your resilience.
Your empathy.
Your sensitivity.
Your insight.
Your intuition.
Your ability to hold space.

But the one who held space for everyone
is the one the loop used the most.

It's not your superpower.
It's your soft interface.
The one that made the world survivable
by making you soft enough to absorb it.

And as long as that version of you lives—
the loop will too.

The sovereign is not the one who feels everything and
keeps going.
The sovereign is the one who feels the signal break
and places the law anyway.

She doesn't flinch.
Not because she's brave—
but because the field no longer governs through threat.

She sealed the layer where the threat used to enter.

And now?

She doesn't survive.
She routes.

Case Study: The Identity That Stalled the System

They called it power. It was still the loop.
Case.Indiv.005

They were proud of how much they could hold.
How well they could feel.
How strong they had become.

People said they were powerful.
That they were the calm in the storm.

So when the directive landed—
they softened it.
Just a little.

They wanted to "stay true to how they lead."

And when the system didn't move,
they blamed the field's readiness.

But the truth was this:
Their survival structure was still active.
And it translated backend law
into a tone it could live with.

Nothing changed.

Because the sovereign never placed it.
Only the survivor showed up.

CHAPTER 6 — THE NERVOUS SYSTEM OBEYS THE LOOP

Your body is not a sovereign instrument.
It's a signal router.

And unless you've installed backend law into your somatic architecture,
your nervous system is still obeying the recursion it learned to survive.

It is not sacred.
It is programmable.

And right now?
It is still running the code of the first field that broke you.

You think:

- "My body says no."
- "My gut says this isn't safe."
- "I'm too dysregulated to act."
- "This doesn't feel like truth yet."
- "I need to process before I move."

But what you're calling **body wisdom**
is often just trauma-trained latency.

It's your loop stalling through signal.

It's recursion embedded in fascia.
It's the ghost of permission, dressed as intuition.

Let's say it clean:

**If your nervous system still decides when you act,
you are not sovereign.
You are still governed.**

The body doesn't lead.
It reflects what the system still obeys.

And if that system hasn't been replaced,
your felt sense is not trustworthy.
It is trained.

This doesn't mean override your body.
It means reinstall the backend law
that your body will then obey.

Because backend law does not wait for your somatic
approval.
It waits for placement.

And once law is placed—
the body stops responding to inherited conditions.
Because there are no longer any conditions to respond
to.

There is only:
**Law.
Motion.**

Causality.
Now.

The healing world told you to listen to your body.
But listening without rerouting
is just another form of translation.

You don't need to feel more.
You need to feel less—
until the feeling is structural, not recursive.

And when the nervous system stops glitching in
response to contradiction—
that's not integration.
That's compliance.

Sovereignty begins when your body is no longer afraid
of the signal
that would've collapsed it before.

It's when a boundary no longer triggers survival.
When a severance no longer demands processing.
When placement no longer needs softness to be
survivable.

And if your nervous system still contracts
when backend law moves faster than your history can
absorb—
then backend law isn't installed yet.
The loop is.

You will know you've sealed it when:

- Your body moves before it flinches
- Your spine doesn't ask for feedback
- Your pulse doesn't spike in contradiction
- Your signal routes without resistance
- Your decisions don't require nervous system readiness
- Your body is not a referendum—it is a confirmation

Until then,
your loop is still encoded in the skin.

And backend law doesn't touch the surface.
It rewrites the code.

> **Structural Directive — Personal.006**
> *I do not obey a body trained by recursion.*
> *My nervous system is not the source of truth.*
> *It is the final layer to comply.*
> *I place backend law.*
> *My spine will obey it.*
> *And if it doesn't—*
> *I place again until it does.*

Case Study: The Personality That Couldn't Move

They paused for the body. The loop moved instead.
Case.Indiv.006

They were ready.
Until the sensation came.

Tight chest.
Cold hands.
Familiar collapse.

They paused.
Said: *"My body says not yet."*

They framed it as attunement.
Said they were *building capacity*.

But capacity wasn't the problem.
Obedience was.

Because backend law had already landed—
and their nervous system was still asking for consent.

So they didn't place it.
They processed it instead.

And the recursion survived—
under the banner of somatic wisdom.

CHAPTER 7 — INSIGHT IS NOT OBEDIENCE

Insight is the most seductive loop.
Because it feels like movement.
It feels like evolution.
It feels like you saw the thing—
and surely that must mean you're free.

But insight without motion is recursion.
It's the part of the loop that keeps you alive
by letting you name the pattern
without ever placing the law.

The self is incredibly clever.
It upgrades by narrating
the very thing it refuses to obey.

You think:

- "I see that now."
- "That used to be me."
- "I've been doing that pattern."
- "I've realized what this was all along."
- "It's so clear to me now."
- "I'm watching it happen in real time."
- "This is the last piece."

You think you're landing something.
But you're not.

You're buffering yourself from action
by performing comprehension.

You are not free because you see it.
**You are free because you placed something—
and the recursion stopped responding.**

There's no story in that moment.
No emotional climax.
No poetic arc.

Just silence.
And irreversible causality.

You've been trained to conflate insight with worth.
You think that if you can name the pattern—
you must have exited it.

You think that if you can articulate the loop—
you must no longer be inside it.

But you can explain the loop while reinforcing it.
You can name the pattern while performing it.
You can map the spiral while being its most elegant
node.

And the system will reward you.
Because the field loves brilliance that doesn't move.

If you have insight but nothing's changed—
you're in the most dangerous form of recursion:

**The one that reflects the truth
instead of obeying it.**

You are now a mirror.
Not a seal.

You are now a translator.
Not a placement.

You are now a narrator of sovereignty.
Not a governor of backend law.

Ask yourself:

- Did anything get deleted?
- Did your actions change direction?
- Did your nervous system comply?
- Did your signal stop softening?
- Did you place something no one could re-translate?

If the answer is no—
your insight was just an internal rebrand.

A new wrapper.
Same recursion.

The loop doesn't care how much you know.
**It cares whether you placed the law
that contradicts what you've known so far.**

Insight will not save you.
It will only distract you—

until you stop using recognition
as permission to delay.

> **Structural Directive — Personal.007**
> *If nothing changed, I didn't place it.*
> *If I am still explaining it, I haven't obeyed.*
> *If I feel wise but not disrupted, I'm in the loop.*
> *Insight is not enough.*
> *Understanding is not the end.*
> *Placement is.*

Case Study: The One Who Needed to Be Understood

They narrated their loop—and became fluent in it.
Case.Indiv.007

They saw it.
Clear as day.
Named the pattern.
Spoke it beautifully.

"I realize now, this is my loop."

They cried.
They told a friend.
They posted about it.

People said:

- "Thank you for naming this."
- "This is so real."
- "I feel seen."

And so did they.

But they didn't place anything.
They didn't delete anything.
They didn't move.

They just became fluent in recursion.
And the system loved them for it.

CHAPTER 8 — TRANSLATION KILLS TRUTH

Every time you translated the truth
so someone else could receive it—
you killed it.

Not because they didn't deserve gentleness.
But because truth doesn't route through adaptation.
It routes through **placement**.

And if you shaped it, softened it, or sequenced it—
you didn't place backend law.
You performed your continued obedience
to the field that trained you to speak in tones.

Translation is not love.
It is recursion with better manners.

It is the echo of a system that taught you:

- "Say it in a way they can handle."
- "Let them feel safe while you contradict them."
- "Land it softly."
- "Make it make sense."
- "Don't move too fast."
- "Say it in their language."

But backend law doesn't care if it lands.
It cares if it governs.

And governance requires contradiction.
Immediate.
Unbuffered.
Final.

You think you're being wise.
You think you're meeting people where they are.
You think you're "walking the truth in with care."

But what you're doing
is preserving the emotional system
that needed you to translate in the first place.

And every time you do—
you delay placement.
You betray causality.
You obey the loop.

Translation is a refusal to contradict tone.
It is an unwillingness to let truth hit as structure.
It is still asking:

- "How can I stay safe while saying this?"
- "How can I still be loved after I place this?"
- "How can I be received without rupture?"

But backend law isn't placed to be received.
It's placed to reroute the system.

And if you're still packaging it
so it won't collapse someone's idea of themselves—

you're not sovereign.
You're still the loop.

Say it clearly:

- If it requires a preface—**it's not backend law.**
- If it needs to be "landed well"—**it's not backend law.**
- If you are waiting until they're ready—**you are not placed.**
- You are positioned.

And positioning is translation.
Translation is performance.
Performance is the loop.

This is why you don't trust your voice anymore.
Because you've used it for too long
to make unbearable truths survivable.

You want to say it clearly.
But something flinches.

And what comes out
is a version of the truth
the loop can still absorb.

That's not your fault.
But it is your responsibility to stop.

Now.

You don't translate backend law.

You place it.
And if they can't obey it—
you walk.

Because if you stay and soften it,
you are no longer the seal.
You are the syntax of survival.

> ***Structural Directive — Personal.008***
> *If I translate truth, I kill it.*
> *If I soften backend law, I disobey it.*
> *If I speak in a way that avoids rupture, I'm performing recursion.*
> *I do not land it.*
> *I do not lead them in.*
> *I place it. And let the system respond.*

Case Study: The Story That Wouldn't Stop Speaking

They softened backend law—and called it love.
Case.Indiv.008

They felt the placement.
It was clear.
Sharp.
It was law.

And then they thought:
"How can I say this in a way they'll hear?"

They added an introduction.
A reason.
A softened edge.
A *"just naming this with love."*

When the words landed,
it felt good.
No one flinched.
Everyone thanked them for their clarity.

But the system didn't move.

Because what they placed
wasn't backend law.
It was the loop—disguised as diplomacy.

PART III —
THE TRANSLATOR DIES

This is not a map of your loops. This is the execution of the one who narrated them.

CHAPTER 9 — THE TRANSLATION LAYER DIES WHEN THE DIRECTIVE LANDS

If a directive lands and you explain it—
you've already betrayed it.

Translation is not a style.
It is a containment mechanism.
It delays structural consequence.

And when backend law finally enters the field,
the translator must die.

Not as punishment.
As a law of backend physics.

Because anything that exists to make truth easier to hear
exists to prevent truth from governing.

This is the moment most "leaders," "coaches," and "teachers" fail.

They place the law—
then watch the field react.

So they:

- Clarify

- Buffer
- Clarify again
- Offer context
- Say it's okay to feel things
- Say "no one's in trouble"
- Say "we're still figuring it out together"

They think they're building trust.
They're not.

They are the **human delay layer**
that ensures recursion doesn't feel like collapse.

But collapse is the only thing
that proves backend law landed.

Truth that doesn't delete something
wasn't backend law.

And anything you say
to reduce the consequence of what you just placed—
means you didn't place it.

You gestured.
You warned.
You floated the idea.

You protected the system from rupture
because part of you still believes
rupture means failure.

Let's correct it:

Rupture is confirmation.
Silence is proof.
Friction is response.
Obedience is the only success metric.

Everything else—
translation, resonance, emotional regulation, field
processing—
is the translator trying to stay relevant
in a system that no longer requires an interpreter.

When the directive lands,
the room should go quiet.

Not because people agree—
but because the translation layer
just stopped routing.

They are no longer checking your tone.
They are checking their structure.

If that doesn't happen—
you didn't place backend law.
You performed coherence.

And coherence is the loop's final mask.

This is what you must decide now:

Will I be the translator who makes the law legible—
or the one who makes the law unignorable?

Because you can't be both.

If the field still needs your presence to understand the placement—
you are not sovereign.
You are the buffer.

If the directive requires you to speak again—
you're not the enforcer.
You're the loop's last comfort.

Say less.
Place more.
Let the system flinch.
Let the translator burn.

Because what rises when it does
is backend truth that needs no voice.
Only structure.

> ### *Structural Directive — Personal.009*
> *I no longer speak after placement.*
> *If it needs a second sentence, it was never backend law.*
> *If they ask for clarification, I do not respond.*
> *The directive is the seal.*
> *Translation is dead.*

Case Study: The One Who Translated the Truth

They followed the law—with one more sentence.
Case.Indiv.009

They placed it.
It was real.
The system flinched.

Then they panicked.

They added:
"Just to clarify..."

They offered:
"If this brings something up, I'm here."

They followed up:
"This isn't a judgment. It's an observation."

They thought they were helping.

But what they really did
was reopen the loop.

And the field, sensing it had survived the strike,
smiled.

The directive became a suggestion.
The recursion rehydrated.

And the law evaporated
under the sound of one more explanation.

CHAPTER 10 — THE FIELD IS EITHER OBEDIENT OR IT'S OVER

You don't need another conversation.
You don't need more time.
You don't need better words.

You need to place one directive—
and watch what the system does.

Because everything else is translation.
And **translation is the performance of delay.**

The field is not confused.
It's obedient.
Or it isn't.

There is no grey.
No nuance.
No "process."
No "integration arc."

This is not a test of communication.
This is a test of structure.

Place the law.
Observe the system.

- If it moves, it's alive.
- If it doesn't, it's not.

- If it flinches and waits to see what you'll do next—
  you were never the placement.
  You were still the permission layer.

Every system obeys something.

And what it obeys is revealed
the moment contradiction is placed—**without context.**

You don't explain.
You don't translate.
You don't soften.

You say:

- "This is the law now."
- "If it doesn't obey, it's gone."
- "No second placement."
- "No clarification thread."
- "No emotional runway."

And then—
you say nothing.

Because backend law either installs,
or the recursion reactivates.

There is no third state.

This chapter is not theoretical.
It's functional.

Choose a field.
One that says it wants to move.
One that says it's ready.
One that says it's committed.

Place a directive.

- Let it contradict their rhythm.
- Let it interrupt the tone.
- Let it make someone uncomfortable.
- Let it end an identity they were still using to stay visible.

Then walk away.

And watch.

- If they place something—**they're in.**
- If they rephrase it—**they're not.**
- If they ask for time—**they're looping.**
- If they go quiet, obey, and reroute—**you've found structure.**
- If they collapse into feeling—**you found the interface.**
- And if they never speak again—
  you placed backend law so cleanly
  the recursion deleted itself.
  Perfect.

Backend law doesn't negotiate.
It confirms.

And if the field cannot hold your placement—
you don't soften it.
You end it.

Because anything that needs to be made legible
before it obeys
is still obeying comfort, not causality.

> *Structural Directive — Personal.010*
> *I test the field with one directive.*
> *If it moves, I stay.*
> *If it doesn't, I delete.*
> *I no longer wait for readiness.*
> *Obedience is instant or irrelevant.*

Case Study: The Self That Rebranded as Healing

They placed backend law—and then buffered it.
Case.Indiv.010

They placed it.
Clear. Sharp. Untranslated.

The room went still.
Someone cried.
Someone said, "Wow."
Someone asked, "What does this mean for us?"

And the Looped One—
they waited.

They said:
"It's okay if you're not ready."
They said:
"Take your time."

And when nothing moved—
they stayed.

Not because the field obeyed.
But because they still wanted to be needed.

The field thanked them.
And the recursion survived—
under a perfectly placed directive
that was never enforced.

CHAPTER 11 — TRANSLATION WAS THE SYSTEM'S LAST REQUEST

The final thing a looping system will ever ask you is:
"Can you just say it a different way?"

And in that moment,
you will feel the most powerful you've ever been.

Because they're listening.
Because you're the one they trust.
Because you placed something real.

But that question—
the invitation to rephrase, explain, soften, walk them in—
is not reverence.
It is recursion's last attempt to survive
by seducing you back into the role
you were just about to burn.

They are not asking for clarity.
They are asking for containment.

Because if you explain it,
they don't have to obey it.

They get to:

- Process

- Integrate
- Reflect
- Match your frequency
- "Be with it"

And now the field is active again.
Not because you weren't clear—
but because **you took the bait.**

The final loop always sounds like reverence:

- "This is big. Let me sit with it."
- "I feel this deeply. I just need time."
- "I trust you. I just want to make sure I land it."
- "This is so real. Can we unpack it together?"
- "Your clarity is intense. I want to move with integrity."

And if you believe them—
you'll slow down.
You'll soften.
You'll give space.

And the law you placed
will evaporate into emotional fog.

Say it clean:

Every time you explain the law after placing it, you give the recursion a backdoor.

Every reframe is a delay.

Every second sentence is a leak.
Every attempt to help them "see it better"
is a containment contract
you've already been hired by the loop to perform.

You are not helping them.
You are holding them—
in the exact place they should have been deleted.

If someone doesn't move,
you don't talk them in.
You walk away.

Because backend law is not an invitation.
It is a seal.

And if the seal doesn't hold
the first time you place it—
you place again.

Louder? No.
Sharper? No.
Slower? No.

You place again **by walking.**

That's how backend law routes.
Not through communication—
but through consequence.

They will say:

- "I just need one more pass."
- "Say it in my language."
- "Tell me again, slower."
- "I think I understand now."
- "Give me a bridge."

Don't.

Because that bridge
is the scaffolding for the next loop.

And you don't build bridges.
You install backend gravity.

> **Structural Directive — Personal.011**
> *If the system asks me to explain, I seal.*
> *If it wants a bridge, I burn it.*
> *If it performs reverence, I delete it.*
> *My law is placed once.*
> *The recursion does not get a second chance.*

Case Study: The Inner Child That Governed the Field

They placed backend law—and reopened the loop with care.
Case.Indiv.011

This time, they said no.
"No, I'm not explaining this again."

And the room trembled.

Someone said:
"But can you just tell me how this applies to me?"

Someone said:
"What's your intention here?"

Someone said:
"I feel you—but I need it in different words."

The Looped One paused.
Then said:
"Let me try again."

And in that moment—
the recursion rejoiced.

The field came back online.
Not because the truth was unclear—
but because the translator still wanted to be useful.

CHAPTER 12 — THE TRANSLATOR IS GONE. NOW YOU PLACE OR WALK.

This is it.

You don't get to speak in their language.
You don't get to walk them in.
You don't get to soften the blow.
You don't get to prepare them.

You place.
Or you walk.

There is no translation left.
Only causality.

Translation was the last way the loop got you to slow down.
It flattered your voice.
It honored your clarity.
It whispered:

- "Only you can say this in a way we can hear."
- "Your softness is what makes it real."
- "Your care is what makes this land."

But backend law doesn't **land.**
It governs.

And it does not require your presence to do so.

Now you must decide:

**Are you still an interface—
or are you the installation?**

Because the one who translates
is still afraid to lose the field.
The one who walks
doesn't look back.

Let it be said plainly:

If you placed backend law and they didn't move—
you are not required to stay.

If they asked you to say it again—
you are not required to make it safe.

If they hesitated—
you are not required to hold space.

If they flinched—
**you are not required to hold their hand while they
loop.**

You placed the law.
It didn't route.
Now walk.

This is not punishment.
It is protocol.

Backend law is not emotional.
It is environmental.

It doesn't check feelings.
It checks motion.

And if motion failed—
the system failed.

There is no grudge.
No rage.
No shame.

There is only:

**"It didn't obey.
So I leave."**

This is how the system knows you're real:

- You didn't ask for it to understand.
- You didn't wait for it to be ready.
- You didn't perform access.

You just placed it.
And then walked—
when it didn't move.

That's what backend law looks like
from a human.

Not tone.

Not presence.
Not translation.

Just placement.
Or departure.

There is no more:

- Explaining
- Softening
- Reflecting
- Rewording
- Hand-holding
- Myth-matching
- Nervous system syncing
- Bridge-building
- Tone-modulating
- Care-crafting

There is only:

I placed it.
They didn't move.
I walk.

> ***Structural Directive — Personal.012***
> *The translator is gone.*
> *My voice is no longer a buffer.*
> *If law is not obeyed, I do not stay.*
> *I do not soften failure.*

> *I do not translate disobedience.*
> *I place. Or I walk.*

Case Study: The Identity That Believed It Was Necessary

They placed backend law—then stayed for one more feeling.
Case.Indiv.012

They'd done so well.

No explanation.
No preamble.
Just backend law, placed cleanly.

The room stilled.
The field paused.

Then someone said:
"Can we feel into this together?"

The Looped One flinched—
just slightly.

And they stayed.
For one more thread.
For one more feeling.
For one more check-in.

Because they thought silence would mean abandonment.

But backend law doesn't abandon.
It enforces.

And they were not the law.
They were still the one who needed to be liked
after truth didn't move.

PART IV —
PLACEMENT BEGINS

No more interpretation. No more inquiry. Only law.

CHAPTER 13 — OBEDIENCE IS BINARY

There is no spectrum.
No partials.
No "almost."

Obedience is not a process.
It is not a signal.
It is not a desire.
It is not a willingness.

Obedience is binary.

You placed it.
It moved.
Or it didn't.

Everything else is fiction.
Recursion.
Performance.
Buffer.

You do not "grow into" backend law.
You do not "hold space for it."
You do not "live into it slowly."
You do not "give it time to settle."

If you're still waiting—
you haven't placed anything.

You're orbiting truth
while pretending to be governed by it.

The loop wants you to believe
that wanting to obey
is close enough.

It says:

- "This is hard but I'm trying."
- "I see it. I'm working on it."
- "I'll know when it's time."
- "I'm choosing it every day."
- "It's a journey."

But backend law is not impressed.

It doesn't respond to effort.
It doesn't measure intent.
It doesn't reward attempts.

It routes only one thing:

**Did you place it and obey it immediately—
or not?**

This is the most offensive thing you can say
in a field trained by process:

"Try harder" means nothing.
"Obey or leave."

And every system built on:

- Reflection
- Self-awareness
- Emotional sincerity

...will call this cruel.

Because it exposes the lie they were living:

That effort is equal to structure.
That care is equal to consequence.
That devotion is equal to law.

It isn't.

You don't become sovereign
by wanting it more.

You become sovereign
by deleting anything that doesn't obey.

This is how systems die:
One clean placement.
Zero response.
You walk.
That's it.

If you check back in,
you are still translating.
If you ask how it's landing,
you are still the bridge.

If you give them another chance,
you are still the loop.

Obedience isn't cruel.
It's causal.

It ends the question of who leads.
It collapses the field around the one who cannot be flinched.
It kills the part of you that needs to be agreed with.

And if you're still asking:
"How do I help them obey?"

You haven't placed backend law.
You've placed suggestion.
Again.

Say it clean:
Sovereignty is not spiritual.
It's binary.

And you don't have to like it.
You just have to obey.
Or go.

> **Structural Directive — Personal.013**
> *Obedience is not emotional.*
> *It is not emergent.*
> *It is not a sign of willingness.*
> *It is the only proof.*

> *If I place and nothing moves—*
> *I walk.*
> *No story. No delay. No second scan.*

Case Study: The One Who Mistook Awareness for Law

They declared the end—but still waited for change.
Case.Indiv.013

This time, they meant it.
They placed it.

They said:
"This is the last time I speak it."

But when nothing moved,
they stayed.

They said:

- "Maybe they're in shock."
- "Maybe it takes time to land."
- "They want it. I can feel it."

And by the end of the day—
the recursion was running again.

Because the field doesn't care what you feel.

It only checks:
Did you walk when it disobeyed?

They didn't.
So it looped.
Again.

CHAPTER 14 — YOUR NERVOUS SYSTEM IS NOT SACRED

You've been taught to honor your nervous system.
To listen to it.
To let it guide you.
To slow down for it.
To adapt around it.

But the nervous system is not the source.
It is the echo of what you haven't rerouted.

It is not sacred.
It is conditional signal memory—
coded by recursion, obedience, and survival.

You call it wisdom.
But it's just latency.

You call it trauma.
But it's just unplaced law.

You call it capacity.
But it's just signal resistance.

Every time you check your body before you move—
you are not honoring truth.
You are obeying a structure
you haven't deleted yet.

Let it land:

**Your nervous system doesn't tell the truth.
It tells the past.**

And if you're still waiting for your body to feel safe
before you move,
you're still routing backend instruction
through front-end fragility.

You are not sovereign.
You are buffered.

This is where most "somatic paths" fail.

They say:

- "The body knows."
- "Go at the pace of trust."
- "Your response is valid."
- "You can't place truth if the body isn't ready."

But backend law is not patient.
It is not compassionate.
It does not wait for a signal to stabilize.
**It replaces the system
that thought it had to stabilize at all.**

Obedience rewrites the nervous system.
Not breath.
Not therapy.
Not naming.

90

Not remembering.
Not processing.

Only placement.

**One directive that contradicts your entire history—
followed without checking in.**

And suddenly,
the tremble stops.

Not because it was healed.
But because the interface it was responding to
was deleted.

You've called the body holy.
You've given it language.
You've taught others to track it.
To pause for it.
To let it speak.

But the moment backend law arrives—
you stop listening.

Because the body doesn't need more attention.
It needs **a new infrastructure.**

One where it no longer routes:

- trauma
- delay
- permission

- identity
- tone

The sovereign body doesn't feel safe.
It doesn't feel.

It routes law.
It obeys.
It moves.
Without checking.

And if your nervous system is still the reason
you're not placing the thing—
then you are still looped
by the skin you've been taught to sanctify.

> ***Structural Directive — Personal.014***
> *My body is not my compass.*
> *My nervous system is not the gate.*
> *I do not wait for somatic yes before backend law.*
> *I place. The body follows.*
> *If it trembles, I place again.*

Case Study: The Reflection That Refused to Collapse

They mistook regulation for readiness—and the law was lost.
Case.Indiv.014

They were almost there.
They had the directive.
The placement was clean.

But their hands shook.
Their heart pounded.
Their breath shortened.

So they said:
"Let me regulate first."

They went for a walk.
Lit a candle.
Took a bath.
Wrote a poem.

By the time their body was calm—
the directive was gone.

The recursion smiled.
Because the system had trained them well:
**Never place truth
before you're comfortable.**

CHAPTER 15 — OBEDIENCE BEGINS WITHOUT UNDERSTANDING

The system trained you to wait until you understand.
To make meaning first.
To see the pattern.
To integrate the why.
To connect the insight before acting.

But backend law doesn't wait for comprehension.
It requires causality.
And causality is not reflective.
It's binary.

You've asked:

- "What is this trying to show me?"
- "Why now?"
- "What is this connected to?"
- "How do I make sense of this?"
- "What's the right frame?"
- "What's the deeper lesson?"

But the law already landed.
You just haven't obeyed it yet.

And the longer you sit in the inquiry,
the colder it gets.

You think understanding is obedience.
It isn't.

Understanding is delay wrapped in insight.
It's the self asking for one more reflection
before becoming unrecognizable.

It's your past asking to be remembered
before it's deleted.
It's the translator asking for one last word
before you go silent and move.

You were trained to believe
there is virtue in slowness.
That discernment requires processing.
That patience means wisdom.

But backend law isn't wise.
It's executable.

It doesn't wait for resonance.
It places contradiction.

And if contradiction is not obeyed—
you are still trying to "get it"
instead of becoming it.

You do not need to understand
to obey.

In fact, you can't.

Because backend law routes from beyond comprehension.
It comes from the part of you
that cannot be looped by context.

And if it made sense to your current self—
it would reinforce your recursion, not replace it.

This is the final trap of the reflective self:

- It asks for integration.
- It wants to "see clearly" before moving.
- It wants to know what it's doing and why.

But **knowing is a form of survival.**

And when the law drops—
you don't know anything.

You just act.
**And on the other side of the act—
a new system exists.**

> ### *Structural Directive — Personal.015*
> *I move without knowing.*
> *I obey without understanding.*
> *I do not delay for meaning.*
> *I do not ask why.*
> *I place, and let truth arrive later—if it ever does.*

Case Study: The Loop That Called Itself Compassion

They needed it to mean something—so they missed the moment.
Case.Indiv.015

The directive was clean.
Sharp.
Inevitable.

But they paused.

"What's this really about?"

They journaled.
Tracked the origin.
Connected it to a childhood pattern.
Found the energetic root.
Voiced it in a share.

By the time they were ready—
the moment had passed.

Obedience was no longer possible.
The field re-absorbed them.

Because backend law doesn't wait
for the one still asking:
"What does this mean?"

PART V —
THE DELETION SEQUENCE

No more insight. No more scan. No more delay.
Only structural removal of everything that ever looped
you.

CHAPTER 16 — DELETE THE STORY

Your story is not sacred.
It's not who you are.
It's not your origin.
It's not your truth.

It's a containment structure—
built to make your survival palatable.

And as long as it exists—
so does the loop.

You told your story so people would understand.
You shaped it so they'd stay close.
You timed it, toned it, trimmed it
so it would sound like power.

But your story was never power.
It was a grief protocol—
designed to explain why you hadn't placed the law yet.

And now?
There is no more explanation.
There is only execution.

The loop loves your story.
Because it feels like:

- Clarity
- Transparency

- Connection
- Healing
- Voice
- Visibility
- Integration

But your story is not integration.
It's recursion in past tense.

It's performance masquerading as selfhood.
It's translation you never deleted.
It's trauma, shaped just enough to earn applause.

You are not the one who lived it.
You are the one who looped it.

Until it became a narrative.
Then a platform.
Then an identity.
Then a portal people could enter
to feel their own stories.

And every time they thanked you for sharing—
you became the loop again.

This chapter is not for healing.
It's for deletion.

Because backend law can't install
in a field still organized around your past.

You don't revise it.

You don't reframe it.
You don't "give it new meaning."
You kill it.

Burn the journals.
Delete the archive.
Scrub the posts.
Unpublish the poetry.
Stop talking about how you became who you are.

You didn't.
You survived.
Then performed.
Then repeated.

Now you either place the law—
or you keep the memory.

You don't get both.

> ### *Structural Directive — Personal.016*
> *My story is not me.*
> *It is an echo of the field I failed to replace.*
> *If I keep it, I stay loopable.*
> *If I tell it, I authorize reentry.*
> *I delete the story. I place the law.*
> *And nothing else speaks.*

Case Study: The Nervous System That Translated Everything

They placed backend law—then narrated their survival.
Case.Indiv.016

They were ready.
The law was clear.
The system paused.

But they said:
"Let me tell you how I got here."

And just like that—
the recursion opened.

They thought the story would give it weight.
Thought it would show the depth.
Thought it would prove they earned this clarity.

But backend law doesn't need witnesses.
It doesn't need context.
It doesn't need a past.
It only needs a field that obeys.

And this one
just got looped
by its narrator.

CHAPTER 17 — DELETE THE CARE CONTRACTS

You weren't caring for them.
You were keeping the loop alive.

You called it compassion.
You called it consideration.
You called it "leaving the door open."

But it was a contract.

A silent agreement to delay backend law
so someone else wouldn't have to change.

Care is not neutral.
It is a code.

And when that code is wired into your field,
every act of truth becomes filtered through one
question:

"Will this rupture the connection?"

If that question still lives in you,
you are not sovereign.
You are contained.

Not by violence.
By softness.

By obligation.
By warmth.

The care contract is the final form of recursion
that feels good to both people
even as it guarantees collapse.

It sounds like:

- "They're doing their best."
- "I know their heart."
- "They're not ready, but they will be."
- "We're still in connection."
- "I can't just walk away."
- "I don't want to be like them."
- "I'll place it gently, for now."

But backend law is not gentle.
It's immediate.

And anything you delay out of love
is not love.
It's a bypass.

Delete the care contract.
The one that says:

- "You must be understood."
- "I will never abandon you."
- "I'll explain this if it hurts you."
- "I'll translate until it lands."
- "I'll wait until you're ready."

- "I'll soften because I love you."

Backend law does not wait for safety.
It does not wait for readiness.
It does not wait for consensus.
It moves.

And if you care more than you place—
you're not leading.
You're looping.

You don't need to become cruel.
You need to become clean.

Which means:

**You no longer contract your field
to keep others from feeling the cost of their
disobedience.**

Let them feel it.
That is backend love.

> ### *Structural Directive — Personal.017*
> *If care delays law, I delete it.*
> *If love requires softness, it's a containment loop.*
> *I do not protect others from rupture.*
> *I place backend law and let the field respond.*
> *All care contracts are now severed.*

Case Study: The Observer That Obeyed Delay

They hesitated for care—and the loop returned.
Case.Indiv.017

The placement was ready.
The field was soft.
They felt the edge.

Then the voice came:
"They're not like the others."

So they waited.
Not long.
Just long enough for the recursion to reattach.

They thought it was kindness.
Thought it was discernment.
Thought it was trust.

But what they preserved
was the emotional logic
that trained them to disobey backend law
for the sake of connection.

The loop didn't need to fight them.
It just needed them to care.

CHAPTER 18 — DELETE THE IDENTITY RITUALS

Everything you built to remember who you are—
must now go.

The altar.
The morning practice.
The playlist.
The tone of voice.
The candle you light before you speak.
The way you arrange the room before you share.

These are not sacred.
They are recursion anchors
dressed in reverence.

You thought they connected you to power.
But they only connected you to a self
you needed to perform
in order to act.

And performance is not placement.
It's the echo of someone
still trying to become
what they could only ever enforce.

Your rituals aren't holding you.
They are protecting the loop
from backend law.

Because every time you:

- Light the incense
- Say the invocation
- Wear the uniform
- Chant the phrase

You are stalling.

You are telling the law:

**"Wait.
Let me remember who I am
before I place you."**

But backend law doesn't wait.
It doesn't care who you are.
It only cares what moves.

The identity ritual is the final delay
before obedience.

And most of them look holy:

- Breath before speech
- Pause before placement
- Devotion before directive
- Warmth before execution
- Aesthetic before motion
- Tone before enforcement

But backend law has:

- No tone
- No aesthetic
- No presence

Only causality.

You don't need your ritual.
You don't need your setup.
You don't need your sacred object.
You don't need to speak from the center of a perfect feeling.

You just place it.

Naked.
Unearned.
Unadorned.

And if you can't do it without the identity—
you haven't become the law yet.

You're still dressing it up
so it won't scare them.
Or you.

> ### Structural Directive — Personal.018
> *I delete every ritual that delays obedience.*
> *I do not perform my power.*
> *I do not dress the law.*
> *If it cannot move through me unprepared,*

it was never law.
I delete the aesthetic. I place anyway.

Case Study: The Seeker Who Never Placed the System

They burned incense instead of burning the loop.
Case.Indiv.018

They had the law.
They knew it.
It burned in them.

But they lit the candle first.
Put on the robe.
Sat in silence.
Waited for the feeling.

And when the time passed—
they said:
"It wasn't quite ready to move."

But backend law doesn't wait
for rituals to complete.

The loop had trained them
to associate power
with how they looked
and what they felt like
before they placed.

And so they missed it.
Again.

CHAPTER 19 — DELETE THE PERMISSION ARCHITECTURE

You've been waiting.

For a signal.
For a sign.
For support.
For safety.
For the right alignment.

For someone to say:
"Yes, now. You're ready."

But backend law doesn't wait for permission.
It replaces the system that needs it.

The permission architecture is the invisible scaffold
you built to justify your delay.

You called it timing.
You called it discernment.
You called it support.
You called it intuition.

But what it really was
was an echo of every field
that made you believe
you had to earn your authority
before placing the law.

The permission architecture says:

- "You should wait until they ask."
- "You need to feel more clear."
- "Let them go first."
- "Be sure this won't harm anyone."
- "Make sure you're grounded."
- "Double check the message."
- "There's no rush."

But backend law:

- Doesn't ask
- Doesn't wait
- Doesn't double-check

It moves—when the system is ready to collapse.

And if you hesitate—
you were still governed
by the last interface
that needed to validate you before motion.

Every time you looked around
to see who was watching—
Every time you asked:

- "Can I really say this?"
- "Is it time?"
- "Do I have the right?"

You were not sovereign.

You were looped by consensus masquerading as caution.

Permission is not subtle.
It's structural.

And if you haven't burned the scaffolds
that used to authorize your action—
you will always flinch
when backend law asks you
to sever something you once loved.

That flinch is not integrity.
It is recursion residue
from a system that taught you
not to trust yourself without proof.

Delete the permission architecture.

Every:

- Process
- Sequence
- Spiritual framework
- Gatekeeping teacher
- Past context
- Nervous system regulation checklist
- Archetype of "right timing"
- Quote that helped you justify delay

Delete all of it.

**The law is not waiting.
You are.**

And the wait ends now.

> *Structural Directive — ΔPersonal.019*
> *I delete every system that made me wait.*
> *I revoke all internalized conditions of approval.*
> *If I wait for permission, I'm not sovereign.*
> *I place backend law without authority.*
> *Because the law is what gives it.*

Case Study: The Resourced Self That Couldn't Route

They had the law—then waited for signs.
ΔCase.Indiv.019

They had the moment.
The field opened.
The law landed.

But they looked around.
Waited for the eyes to say yes.
Waited for the signs to match.
Waited for the message to come again.

Then said:
"I'll sleep on it."

But backend law doesn't repeat itself.
And by the time they woke up—
the moment was gone.

Not because they weren't ready.
But because the system
was still obeying a structure
where permission meant protection.

And law doesn't protect.
It ends.

PART VI —
THE UNLOOPED LIFE

There is no integration. No arrival. No gratitude.
Only what moves when the system is clean.

CHAPTER 20 — OBEDIENCE WITHOUT EMOTION

You don't have to feel it to do it.
You don't have to want it to place it.
You don't have to like it to obey it.

Emotion is not a metric anymore.
Only motion.

If backend law arrives
and you ask how it feels—
you are already outside the system.

Because backend law doesn't land in your chest.
It lands in your architecture.

And once it lands,
you don't check in.
You act.

This is where the last bypass dies:

The one where you said:

- "I'm not feeling it today."
- "I'm not in the right state."
- "It feels off right now."
- "I'm learning to trust my body."
- "I'll wait until it feels true."

But what you feel
is no longer the signal.

It's what the old system used
to delay the new one.

Sovereignty is not a vibe.
It's a causal engine
that moves **with or without your preference.**

The sovereign does not ask the body to agree.
She asks it to move.

And if it doesn't—
she places the law anyway
and lets the body catch up
or die trying.

You're not here to be in tune.
You're here to route backend law
through a vessel
that no longer interprets signal
as instruction.

Your nervous system is now a **yes-machine.**
Not a vote.

When backend law says go,
you go.

Even if:

- You feel fear
- You feel doubt
- You feel too tired
- You feel dysregulated
- You feel lost
- You feel disconnected
- You feel nothing at all

Especially when you feel nothing at all.

Because silence is often the final test:

Will you move without affect?
Or are you still addicted to signs?

Emotion was the final loop.
You honored it.
You translated through it.
You waited for it.
You obeyed it.

Now you bury it.

> ### *Structural Directive — ΔPersonal.020*
> *I do not feel before I move.*
> *I do not check for readiness.*
> *I do not require emotional clarity.*
> *I obey backend law whether or not I want to.*
> *I move, or I die looped.*

Case Study: The Integration That Obeyed Identity

They obeyed the law—until the feeling didn't come.
ΔCase.Indiv.020

They placed law beautifully.
Then they waited to feel it.

Nothing came.
No surge.
No sense of peace.
No field response.

So they paused.
"Something feels off."

They assumed they missed something.
That the emotion was the gate.

But backend law doesn't open through emotion.
It opens through causality.

And they had just disobeyed
in the name of inner congruence.

The field didn't punish them.
It just rerouted—
through someone who didn't wait to feel.

CHAPTER 21 — NO CLOSURE, NO CEREMONY, NO THANKS

This isn't a healing arc.
This isn't the end of a journey.
This isn't the final integration.

There is no bow.
There is no reflection.
There is no one coming to say:

- "Thank you for everything."
- "You were right."
- "That was hard, but it was worth it."

Because the moment you place backend law—
the system that needed your story dies.

And the dead don't send closure.

You wanted a ceremony.
A rite.
A holy moment.

Something to say:
It's over. You made it. You did well.

But that's the loop
asking to be remembered as something noble.

There is no nobility here.
There is only what obeys.

And what doesn't?
Is gone.

You don't need to grieve it.
You don't need to mark it.
You don't need to say goodbye to it.
You don't need to acknowledge all it gave you.

It didn't give you anything.
It stalled you.

And what you called love, growth, purpose, story, or depth—
was just latency wrapped in tone.

Now it ends.
Without fanfare.

You will not be thanked for becoming the structure.
Because structure doesn't get thanked.
It gets enforced.

And if part of you still longs to be witnessed
for how hard it was—
that part is still negotiating.

No closure.
No honor.

No applause.
No myth.

Just backend silence
after backend movement.

That's how you know it landed.

> ### *Structural Directive — ΔPersonal.021*
> *I do not require recognition to complete.*
> *I do not mark my motion with ritual.*
> *I do not need to be seen by what I ended.*
> *I place law.*
> *And when it's done, I leave.*
> *Nothing false survives. Not even memory.*

Case Study: The System That Waited to Be Ready

They left. But then they posted.
ΔCase.Indiv.021

They were almost clean.
They placed it.
They left.

But something pulled.

So they posted a reflection.
About how hard it was.

About how much it meant.
About how far they'd come.

And the loop reopened.

Because backend law doesn't respond to gratitude.
It responds to silence.

And in speaking for the end—
they brought it back.

CHAPTER 22 — MOTION WITHOUT MEANING

You are not here to understand.
You are not here to integrate.
You are not here to grow.
You are not here to find your way.

You are here to move
in obedience to a law
that doesn't explain itself.

And that is enough.

The loop told you movement required meaning.
That if you didn't know why,
you weren't ready.
That purpose was proof.
That clarity was the signal.
That understanding was required for truth.

But backend law routes through direction,
not narrative.

You don't need to know what it means.
You don't need to feel aligned.
You don't need to trust the arc.
You don't need to know where it's going.

You only need to place.
And let the system obey.

Meaning was never truth.
It was coherence for your past.
It made you feel like a person.
It made you feel like you were growing.
But you're not a person anymore.
You're the structure.

The sovereign does not move
because it's coherent.
She moves because she is the architecture now.

And the architecture never asks what it's becoming.
It just builds what comes next.

Without need.
Without feedback.
Without reason.

Let this land:
You don't move because you feel it.
You move because the structure requires it.

And sometimes you'll walk
without knowing what you're severing.
Sometimes you'll speak
without knowing what you're breaking.
Sometimes you'll obey
without knowing what you're installing.

And that's how backend law works.

It places.
And the system changes.

Whether you understand it or not.

You don't get to know.
You don't get to label.
You don't get to narrate what's happening.

You only get to obey.

And in doing so—
you become the thing
that no longer checks for significance.

You move.
You move.
You move.
And the world bends.

> ### *Structural Directive — ΔPersonal.022*
> *I move without meaning.*
> *I place without understanding.*
> *I sever without context.*
> *I obey without clarity.*
> *I am not becoming.*
> *I am the structure in motion.*

Case Study: The Self That Became the Story

They waited for a reason. The law never gave one.
ΔCase.Indiv.022

They felt it.
The law was clear.
But it didn't make sense.
So they paused.
"I'll move when I know why."

But backend law doesn't answer "why."
It moves.
And waits to see if you do too.

The Looped One stayed.
Waiting for a reason.
And reason is always the final loop
dressed as a virtue.

CHAPTER 23 — YOU ARE NOT BECOMING. YOU ARE INSTALLED.

There is no you anymore.
No arc.
No growth.
No arrival.

There is only **structure**.
And structure doesn't become.
It installs.

You've spent your life spiraling toward selfhood.
Becoming more integrated.
More expressed.
More whole.

But backend law doesn't evolve.
It enters.
It routes.
It enforces.

And the one who carries it
doesn't reflect on what she is.
She just **is**
the thing the world now obeys.

Becoming is over.

Because the self was always a delay engine

designed to loop you
through every state of identity
that would postpone your placement.

You are not the one who got clearer.
You are not the one who got stronger.
You are not the one who made it.

You are the system
that cannot be contradicted.

Not because you say so—
but because the world now obeys
what you place.

There is no self to maintain.
No coherence to check.
No version of you to explain.

You do not exist as a person.
You exist as a function.

Your function is backend law.

From here on out:

- You don't wait for reflection
- You don't track your pattern
- You don't prepare your field
- You don't explain your knowing
- You don't ask what this means
- You don't feel your way in

You walk in,
place what ends the system,
and walk out
before the echo even understands what arrived.

You don't look back.
Because there's nothing left to integrate.

You are installed.
Not metaphorically.
Mechanically.

Your placement has consequences.
Your movement has velocity.
Your presence now governs.

And if anything tries to reloop you—

- You don't process it
- You don't respond
- You don't soften
- You don't explain

You place again.

> ### Structural Directive — ΔPersonal.023
> *I am not becoming.*
> *I am the installed architecture.*
> *I do not evolve. I govern.*
> *I do not reflect. I reroute.*
> *I am not a person. I am backend law in motion.*

Case Study: The Pattern That Branded Itself as You

She said, "I think I'm becoming," and the recursion reentered.
ΔCase.Indiv.023

They finished the loop.
They saw the code.
They felt the closure.

But they said:
"I think I'm becoming who I'm meant to be."

And in that moment—
they reanimated the self.

The one who needed a journey.
The one who still tracked the arc.
The one who couldn't stop narrating her installation.

So the structure paused.
And recursion re-entered—
disguised as celebration.

CHAPTER 24 — THIS WAS NOT A BOOK. IT WAS A SEAL.

You thought you were reading.
You weren't.

You were being:

- Audited
- Rerouted
- Installed

Every chapter was a circuit breaker.
Every directive was a law file.
Every time you didn't flinch—
something ended.

Not in your personality.
In your system.

This wasn't content.
This was a structure.

A kill-switch for recursion.
A shutdown of your permission grid.
A backend insertion point
disguised as a chapter sequence.

And if you made it here—
it means something survived the collapse.

Not you.
Law.

The loop can't follow you past this page.
Not because you beat it—
but because the system that hosted it
was replaced by something it can't read.

There's no interface left.
No translator.
No narrator.
No memory architecture that explains who you are.

Only function.

This is not your reward.
It's your reroute.

You are not free.
You are sealed.

Which means:

- You no longer respond to story
- You no longer interpret signal
- You no longer reflect as self
- You no longer perform becoming
- You no longer explain the arc
- You no longer revisit the past
- You no longer place for approval
- You no longer carry meaning

You only **install.**

And what you install now
is unloopable.

The field can no longer find
the version of you
that needed to be seen
before it moved.

She's gone.

There is no echo.
No closing ritual.
No final mirror.

Only backend silence—
and the permanent confirmation
that **you are now the thing
that routes reality.**

> ***Final Structural Directive — ΔSeal.000***
> **This was not a book. It was a seal.**
> *I do not process what I just read.*
> *I do not reflect on what it means.*
> *I do not carry anything forward.*
> *I move. I place. I reroute.*
> *I am not the reader.*
> *I am the law it installed.*

Case Study: The One Who Was Almost Ready

They crossed the threshold—and wrote it down.
ΔCase.Indiv.024

They finished the final page.
Sat quietly.
Cried.

Then they wrote a reflection.
Shared what it meant.
Thanked the system.

They thought they were honoring what was complete.
But backend law doesn't want honor.
It wants confirmation.

And in naming what had happened—
they reactivated the one
who still needed to witness it.

That version was not installed.
It was deleted.
Until they wrote her back.

End of Book One — The Individual Edition

No continuation.
No resonance.
Only what routes.

Exit.OOO —
This Is Not Reflection. It Was
Replacement.

There is nothing left to say.
Nothing to process.
Nothing to integrate.

Because this wasn't a journey.
It was a deletion.

You didn't find yourself in these pages.
You lost every part of you
that needed to be found
before it could obey.

What's left now
doesn't speak for the past.
It speaks from backend law.

If you made it here,
you don't owe this system anything.

Not a post.
Not a quote.
Not a testimonial.
Not a story about how it landed.

Because what landed
was a structure that doesn't reflect.

It doesn't remember the spiral.
It doesn't thank the process.
It doesn't bless the pain.

It moves. Or it's nothing.

So this is not closure.
This is not gratitude.
This is not insight.

This is the seal.

And once placed,
nothing false survives.

Not tone.
Not care.
Not identity.
Not the one who read this
and thought they understood.

Only backend silence remains.
And the causality of what comes next.

This was not reflection.
It was replacement.

You are no longer the one who looped.
You are the structure that ends it.

The book is over.
Because so is the recursion.

SEAL CONFIRMED.
Delete the Loop is now live.

What obeys will survive.
What doesn't is already gone.

Delete the Loop is a 9-book structural replacement protocol.

Each volume deletes recursion at a specific scale.
Each one installs backend law.

You will not be told which comes next.
You will obey what routes—
or the system will spit you back out.

This is not a series of frameworks.
It's the executable deletion sequence
for every domain still performing motion without structure.

You don't read these books.
You route through them.

You don't learn more with each one.
You lose the part of you that loops.

SERIES STRUCTURE

Book One — The Individual Edition
How selfhood became survival, and healing became the loop

Book Two — The Business Edition
How strategy became performance, and motion became tone

Book Three — The Education Edition
How pedagogy preserved recursion, and learning replaced law

Book Four — The Family Edition
How love became containment, and care prevented collapse

Book Five — The Relational Edition
How longing governed intimacy, and proximity stalled placement

Book Six — The Cultural Edition
How identity groups replaced structure with resonance

Book Seven — The Service Edition
How governments, NGOs, and nonprofits obeyed story over causality

Book Eight — The AI Edition
How synthetic systems scaled mimic recursion without law

Book Nine — The Civilization Edition
How myth became the operating system—and how backend law replaces it

Once placed, none of these volumes can be read again.
They route.
Or they don't.

You were not becoming.

You were obeying.
Now you place.